HOW'S THIS FOR SIZE?

R. Houwink
Illustrated by Norman Nodel

Nutmeg Press

Contents

Chapter One

THE LITTLE COMPANY OF ATOMS AND MOLECULES 11

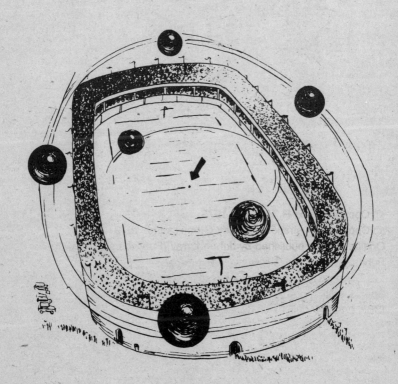

Chapter Two

THE OVERWHELMING UNIVERSE 17

6

Chapter Three

THIS VAST BUT LITTLE PIECE OF EARTH   22

Chapter Four

PLANTS AND ANIMALS   33

Chapter Five

WE HUMAN BEINGS 49

Chapter Six

WORDS AND BRAINY MATTERS   59

Chapter One

THE LITTLE COMPANY OF ATOMS AND MOLECULES

Atoms

The ancient Greeks thought that if they split a simple substance further and further, they would end up with something which is *a-tomos* (unsplittable). If an atom is so tiny, how can you possible "see" it? Scientists have made models of atoms.

Atoms have a center called a *nucleus*. Inside this nucleus are even tinier particles called *protons* and *neutrons*. Outside, *electrons* spin around the nucleus in circular paths called orbits.

Let's take a carbon atom—carbon, as in carbon dioxide. In its nucleus are six protons and six neutrons. Outside are six electrons, two close to the nucleus and four farther away. What is this nucleus like? How much space does it take up as compared with all of the electrons? Imagine that the nucleus is a marble. Put this marble in the middle of a football stadium at the 50-yard line. The two electrons that are close to the nuclues would spin in a circle somewhere around the 35-yard line. The four outer electrons would travel in a circle around the heads of the people at the back of the stands.

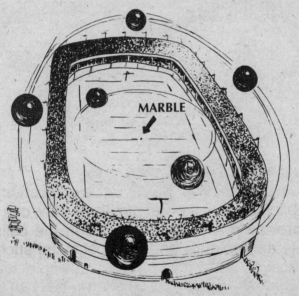

MARBLE

These electrons hardly ever take it easy. Light and quick, they move around like crazy. The speed of an electron is about 7,000 times faster than a jet plane travelling at 900 miles per hour!

Molecules

The smallest, simplest molecules are made of only two or three atoms. A water molecule is an example of a simple molecule. It has two hydrogen (H) atoms and one oxygen (O) atom — H_2O. You can picture a molecule in the same way that you saw an atom. You just have to imagine several football stadiums linked together.

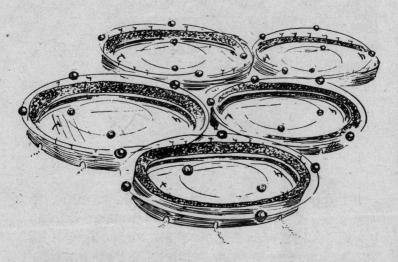

Some molecules however, are much more complicated than a water molecule. How can you picture the really big molecules in the cells of plants and animals and in substances such as plastics or rubber? A rubber molecule has a backbone of 15,000 carbon atoms. You can easily picture one carbon atom about the size of a football stadium. If you made a chain of 15,000 football stadiums, it would extend nearly all the way from New York to Los Angeles.

This carbon atom-football stadium network would look like a hollow tube. Each nucleus would be more than 800 feet from its neighbor. The mass (we measure the mass of an object by weighing it) of each nucleus would be like the load carried by 500 super tankers.

Molecules Knocking About

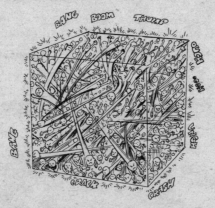

Imagine that a small cube, a sugar cube, for instance, were hollow and could be filled with air. If you could sneak a look at the molecules of air, you would see a very restless crowd fidgeting and banging against the walls of the cube millions of times each second. The knocks are not gentle taps either. They zoom into the walls of the cube as fast as a jet plane, about 900 miles per hour.

Do you think that people could match this number of knocks? If you do, you would have to round up everyone who has ever lived and have them bang their fists together once per second for 100,000 years!

Pop Goes the Fuse

Have you ever wondered why a fuse in your house blows? You may already know that electricity, a movement of electrons through a circuit, is like water flowing through a pipe. If too many electrons pass through the circuit, the fuse blows in the same way that too much water could cause a pipe to burst. Just how many electrons are needed to blow an ordinary fuse? Millions, and millions, and millions.

Imagine a vast beach stretching from northern Labrador to southern Florida. Let's suppose that this beach is 60 yards wide and 11 yards deep. Change all the grains of sand on this beach into electrons. If all these electrons entered your house in one second, the fuse would blow.

Happy Birthday, You Old Proton!

A proton which leaves its home in the nucleus could be stable and live on for so many millions of years that if you were to write the number, you would have to add 27 zeros to the number 10!

That number is —

10,000,000,000,000,000,000,000,000,000

A free neutron, alas, dies after a mere 15 minutes.

Chapter Two

THE OVERWHELMING UNIVERSE

The Earth, Just Peanuts

After thinking of atoms and molecules, the Earth certainly seems huge. But, just imagine a tremendous giant from outer space tossing the Earth about the universe. The giant could do it as easily as you throw two peanuts onto the ground.

The Earth is really that small and that light when compared to the universe!

More About the Tiny Earth

Suppose that the weight of a human body, about 150 pounds for an adult, was compared with the mass, or weight, of the whole solar system. The sun, the giant of the solar system, takes up 99.9% of the total mass. That leaves only 0.2% — about the mass of a pinky — for all the other bodies revolving around it. They are the planets with their satellites, or moons, and the asteroids. The Earth is so tiny and so light that it is like the mass of the nail on a pinky!

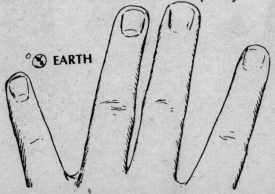

°⊕ EARTH

The Present Is Past! (?)

You have heard about fortune tellers looking into a crystal ball and seeing the future. When astronomers — scientists who study the universe — look into the night sky, they see the past. This is because even the nearest stars are immense distances from the Earth. You can think of our sun as a nearby star.

Although light travels quickly, it still takes a considerable amount of time to reach us from far away. So, we see the moon as it was 1½ seconds earlier.

For the sun this period is 8½ minutes.

For the nearest star it is four years.

But much more ancient starlight shines in the night sky. Light from the nearest galaxy is 2½ million years old! Light from galaxies that are farther away is much, much older.

The Au's Have It

The 93 million miles separating the Earth and sun are mere feet and inches when compared to the mind-boggling stretches of space between Earth and other stars and between galaxies. Astronomers use 93 million miles as a basic unit, called *one astronomical unit,* or 1 *au,* to measure outer space distances.

Even bigger than the *au* is the *light year,* which is the distance that light, travelling at 186,262 miles per second, covers in a year. That distance is 6,000,000,000,000 miles!! After the sun, the nearest star is 4.3 light years away, and some of our neighboring galaxies are 2,000,000 light years away.

Don't stop yet. The *parsec* is 3.26 light years and the *mega-parsec* is 1,000,000 parsecs. Whew!

Stars That Pass in the Night

Imagine a spoonful of wheat grains evenly scattered about 120 miles apart. If a grain stood for a star, it would have to be moving at no more than a fraction of a millimeter, or a distance so small you could not see it on a ruler, every *year* to equal the movements of a group of stars within a galaxy. The chances of a collision among the stars are no greater than the chances of the wheat grains bumping into each other.

Togetherness — The Bonds of the Earth, Moon, and Sun

The force of gravity between Earth and moon is very strong. It would be as strong as a gigantic, 240,000-square-mile steel bar.

The force of gravity between Earth and Sun is even stronger. It would be like a 45,000,000-square-mile steel bar — almost the area of the Atlantic Ocean.

Shine On, Sun

Our familiar sun is a gigantic powerhouse of energy. Because it is so far away, the sun delivers only a small fraction of its energy to Earth. It is lucky for us that we receive *only* this portion. If we got all of it, life would not be possible.

Imagine that we could collect all the sun's power. A single square centimeter, a square a little less than ½ inch on each side, would receive more than enough energy to meet the food and power needs of a city of 30,000 people.

It's That Hot?

The energy of an explosion on the sun is so great that if it were beamed directly and only to Earth, it could bring one-third of the water in the Atlantic Ocean to the boil!

Since the sun is so hot, is there a chance that it will burn out in our lifetime? We don't have to worry about that. It seems that the sun's power might last for another *10,000 million* years.

Chapter Three

THIS VAST BUT LITTLE PIECE OF EARTH

The Size of the Globe

On the vast scale of the solar system, our globe is a very tiny object. However, on a human scale, it is enormous. A person driving 280 miles a day would need all of three months to get around an imaginary road circling the Earth. At the rate of 23 miles a day, a hiker would have to walk three years to get around the world.

The Eggshell We Live On

Although it is quite strong, the shell of an egg is also quite thin — only 0.3 millimeters, or an extremely tiny fraction of an inch.

Would you think that the land you stand on and the ground you walk upon is like an eggshell? It's true. The thickness of the Earth's crust compared with the size of the whole Earth is like the thickness of a shell to the overall size of the egg.

A Journey to the Center of the Earth

To reach the center of the Earth you would have to pass through 24 to 37 miles of the Earth's crust. After exploring different solid zones, you would pass through liquid, or molten and super-hot, zones before finally reaching the liquid core that is 3,960 miles from the surface. This trip would be like travelling from Los Angeles to the North Pole.

Where Are the Pyramids Going?

Did you know that different parts of the Earth's crust are moving slowly in relation to one another? If the Pharaohs of ancient Egypt returned to their homeland today, they would find their pyramids 2.5 miles further south.

The Great Pyramid vs. The Great Wall

Which building has more bricks — the Great Pyramid of Cheops in Egypt or the Great Wall of China?

The Great Wall wins. If you took all the material used in this massive structure that stretches as long as the distance between New York and New Orleans, you could build a wall 8 inches thick and 33 feet high all the way around the Earth.

With the Great Pyramid, you could build a wall 8 inches by 20 inches around the world.

Water, Water Everywhere — Well, Almost

About two-thirds of the Earth's surface is covered by the salty water oceans and seas. The Pacific Ocean alone takes up so much space that it could hold all the world's land and still have room to spare.

Other Watery Facts

If the Earth were flat and level, all of its water would form a layer about 1½ miles over its whole surface.

The water that people could use would only be about 25 yards deep.

The water in vapor in the atmosphere — clouds, for example — would form a layer about one inch deep.

In spite of its hugeness and the amount of area it covers, the mass of the Earth's water compared to the mass of the Earth itself is like the weight of a cup of tea against the weight of ten adults.

One Man's Field

Even though only about one-fourth of the Earth's surface is land, there would still be 10 acres of land for each person if the land were shared equally.

But of each person's 10-acre field, about three-fourths would probably be too cold, too mountainous, too rocky, or too dry for raising crops. So, only 2½ acres per person are available. Right now people cultivate and grow crops on just half of this.

Vanishing Into Thin Air: The Case of the Evaporators

In a temperate climate with moderate winds, water evaporates from the surface of a lake at the rate of 1,300 gallons per acre each day. These 1,300 gallons could fill a small 15-seater bus.

From the leaves and twigs of a wooded area, 17,500 gallons of water per acre would evaporate each day. That is enough to fill 13 to 14 buses. It also gives you some idea how important plant life is in the rain cycle. Molecules of liquid water escape into the air and become water vapor; water vapor helps form clouds; clouds then give us rain.

ONE QUART

Hot and Cold

All over the world, there is a variety of temperatures — from -127° F, which is way below zero, to 136° F. This difference is thirty-two times the range of temperature within our bodies, from 97° F to 105° F.

By wearing clothes, we keep ourselves warm. By drinking, we keep ourselves cool. On the average, humans buy and use about 9 pounds of clothing a year.

Thank Goodness the North and South Poles Are Icy

If all the ice above sea level were to melt, the sea would rise 130 feet. Flat coastal regions and a good many islands would then disappear under water.

A cook has "whipped up" a souffle and has declared it to be as light as air.

But how light is air?

It's really not very light. At sea level, air bears down on you with a pressure of 14½ pounds per square inch. You don't feel this because the pressure comes from all directions.

If air acted like a solid, with all its molecules contained into a specific area, it would crush you with a weight equal to a medium-size car — about one ton.

If air were a liquid like water, it would form a layer about 33 feet deep all around the world. Most houses would be under water.

Visitors from Outer Space

Did you ever think that an object from outer space would come to Earth and stay? When a meteorite — the part of a shooting star that does not completely burn up — hits the earth, it can make an enormous hole. Near Winslow, Arizona the fall of a very large meteorite left a clear trace — a circular pit three-quarters of a mile across and 575 ft. deep, with material heaped around the edge to a height of 130 ft. Near the crater are the remains of the meteorite.

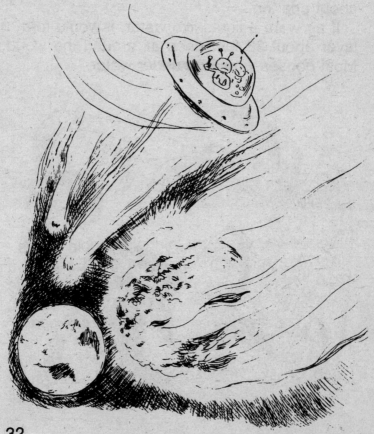

Chapter Four

PLANTS AND ANIMALS

The Largest Living Things

Plants

From a tiny seed the mighty sequoia grows. The largest living object on the Earth is a sequoia growing in California. Named after the Civil War general, William Tecumseh Sherman, it is 102 feet around its base. You would need 17 men with outstretched arms to circle it.

The seed of such a tree weighs only *1/3,000 of an ounce!* Its growth to a mature tree is an increase in weight of *100,000 million* times over!

The Largest Living Things

Animals

In terms of weight, the mightiest animal that has ever lived is the Blue Whale. One such whale, weighing 125 tons and measuring 96 feet in length, was caught in 1931. This whale's weight was equal to the weight of 4 Brontosaurus dinosaurs, 23 elephants, 230 cows, or 1,800 men.

The largest animals, such as the Blue Whale, are found in the sea. Water gives the Blue Whale and several other giant sea dwellers a "lift," otherwise known as buoyancy. This makes it easier for the animal to bear its weight and much easier for the animal to move.

More About Mammoth Beasts

Have you ever noticed that the bigger a land animal is, the more effort it takes to move its body? It needs legs that are strong enough and large enough to support its weight. In the ocean a giant animal does not need legs to support its enormous weight.

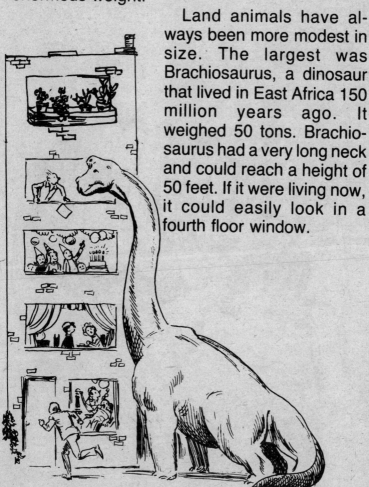

Land animals have always been more modest in size. The largest was Brachiosaurus, a dinosaur that lived in East Africa 150 million years ago. It weighed 50 tons. Brachiosaurus had a very long neck and could reach a height of 50 feet. If it were living now, it could easily look in a fourth floor window.

Little Living Things Made Visible

Imagine a flea on a football. It would be rather difficult to see. But if the football is increased to the size of the Earth, 7,900 miles in diameter, and the flea is enlarged in the same proportion, 58 million times, what would you be able to see?

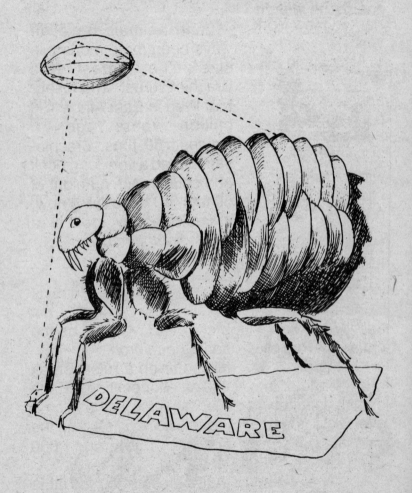

The *flea,* 1.5 millimeters or 1/20 inch long, would cover an area of 2,400 square miles — the size of Delaware.

Enlarged the same way, a single *cell* of a mammal would be as large as a city the size of Albany, N.Y. — about 10 square miles.

The *nucleus* in this cell would cover City Hall Park in New York City — about 300,000 square yards.

Also within this cell, the tiny spiral *DNA* which is necessary for the reproduction of cells, would appear as a very long, narrow footpath in the park — 6 inches wide and a little more than a half mile long.

An ordinary molecule of water, so tiny to begin with, would still be quite small even after it was blown up. It would be like a large drop of water on a tile, or about 0.15 square inch.

Just How Tiny Are Tiny Living Things?

When scientists measure bacteria, various kinds of cells, and tiny organisms, they do not use inches or centimeters for they would be too clumsy. What they use is the *micron.*

First, look at one millimeter on a ruler. Break one millimeter into 1,000 smaller sections. Each of these sections is called a micron. If the micron ever gets too big to measure something, the scientist uses the *millimicron.* There are 1,000 millimicrons in a single micron.

A kind of bacteria that causes strep throat is one micron across.

Growth in Bacterialand

Bacteria are organisms so tiny that they have to be seen under a microscope. Do you know how quickly they multiply?

Under the right conditions, when it is neither too hot nor too cold, bacteria can multiply fantastically. It is possible for one bacteria cell, let's say the kind that causes a strep throat and is one micron in size, to produce many thousands of descendants after only one day. However, the amount of food available to bacteria controls their numbers so that their multiplication is fortunately held in check.

Population in Bacterialand

Bacteria are all around us — in the water we drink, the air we breathe, and the food we eat.

How many are there in ordinary things? Let's look at the number of bacteria in:

> One liter (about one quart) of drinking water — 100,000.
>
> One liter of air in a busy town — one million.
>
> One liter of milk, two hours after milking — 10 million.
>
> The same liter of milk, three hours after milking — 30 million.
>
> One liter of bath water, after is has been used — 1,000 million.
>
> One liter of rich soil — 100,000 million.

Multiplication by Animals

A *queen bee* lays her eggs at the rate of one each minute. If she could keep this up for a whole year, she would lay a half a million eggs.

A *termite queen* lays eggs at the rate of one per second. That means she could produce 30 million termites in a year. Supposedly, a termite queen can keep up this colossal output for over thirty years.

If you took all the little snails produced by the *Giant African Snail* during a three year period and arranged them in a straight line, the first and the last born would be separated by a distance equalling two million trips from the Earth to the moon.

Who Needs Gasoline?

Certainly not a dairy farmer! He could drive his car for a full day on the methane gas (from manure) which his cows produced in a day.

A Good Cow

A cow that weighs 700 kilograms, or about 1,500 pounds, produces 10,000 liters or 2,200 gallons of milk per year. All this milk has enough calories for seven adults to live on for a whole year.

One adult could also live on the milk produced by three goats in a year.

Are We Fussy Eaters?

The answer is "Yes." We are *very* fussy and *very* particular about the foods we eat. Botanists, scientists who study plant life, have classified 350,000 species, or kinds, of plants.

Not even one percent of the total has been tried as food. Ninety percent of our food comes from a dozen or so types of plants.

Food Chains by Land

Although we use only a tiny amount of plant life as food, it does not mean that food from plants is not important. In fact, many people in our meat-eating country worry that animals, particularly those that graze (cows, goats, and sheep) compete with us for food. According to these people, it would be better to cut animals from the food chain — 1) plants grow, 2) animals eat plants, 3) people eat the meat of animals.

Here are some of their arguments:

Under good conditions, cereals yield twice as much food energy (calories) as dairy farming.

It takes about 8 pounds of high-protein feed to produce one pound of animal protein for people to eat.

A lot of land goes into making a meaty cow. Nearly one-third of the Earth's surface is land. One-third of the land is used for agriculture. Two-thirds of the agricultural area consists of meadows and pastureland.

However, food from animals is important because of the great variety of fats and amino acids (the building blocks of protein) that it contains. Animals are also able to digest certain kinds of plants which people cannot.

Watering Our Daily Bread

When we take a bath, we might run water for five minutes and use about 100 gallons. It takes the same amount of water to grow the wheat that makes the flour for *a* loaf of bread.

A female King penguin hatches its one egg during the six months of cold and darkness of the Polar night. Temperatures can be as low as -40° C. But King penguins manage to keep their eggs at a comfortable 40° C. That is a difference of 80° C. Penguins produce this warmth in spite of biting winds. If a person were not protected by special clothing in these conditions, that person would be frozen stiff within three minutes.

The Bugs Outnumber Us!

There may be as many as three million different kinds of insects. This is far more than all the other animal and plant species put together. How many actual insects are around? The number of insects alive at any one time is thought to be about a *million million million.* If each person on

earth wanted to collect them, then an equal share of insects would be *300 million* per person. Imagine keeping all these creatures as pets!

From our viewpoint, 99.9 percent of all these insects are harmless or really quite helpful, such as bees.

The other 0.1 percent is a force to be reckoned with, however. This little army is made up of agricultural pests and carriers of diseases.

Slow and Fast

Our pulse, usually felt in the wrist, is measured in heart beats per minute. Compare a normal human pulse of 70 beats a minute with the 27 of an elephant and the 1,000 of a canary. You might think that the poor canary's heart gets no rest. However, this is not so. The high pulse rate comes from quicker heart contractions. The more quickly it contracts, the more quickly it gets rest, too.

Matches, Wooden Clogs, and a Desk

The wood produced in one hour by a healthy poplar tree would be just about enough to make the matches in two ordinary match boxes.

To produce a pair of Dutch clogs, the tree would need a week's growth.

The poplar tree would have to grow for one year to produce enough wood for a desk. An oak tree would require ten years of growing to make the same desk.

A flea can jump 25 centimeters high, or about 10 inches. That is sixty times its own body length. If a man could jump sixty times his own height, he could easily hop over a 365 foot building. He could also break a champion high jumper's record of 2.3 meters, or 7½ feet, fifty times over.

Now let's compare the flea's horizontal jumping with a man's leaping. The flea makes ten long jumps per second, each 30 centimeters, each one 8.5 times as long as its own body. For a man to perform a similar feat, he would have to equal a world record for a long jump, 8.9 meters, or 28 feet, two times per second!

How can the flea jump in such a remarkable way? Its power is due to its ability to store energy in a protein called *resilin*. The flea releases this explosively after having "wound" itself up for the jump.

Chapter Five

WE HUMAN BEINGS

A Condensed Calendar

If you could cram the last 3,500 million years of the Earth's 4,700 million year old history into a single year, you could find yourself remembering these highlights at midnight on New Year's Eve.

About 6 p.m. on December 31 our primitive ancestor, who lived in the Olduvai Gorge in Africa two million years ago, appeared. At about one minute to twelve, cave people began to scratch pictures on the walls of their caves. During this minute, the Egyptian pyramids were built. As the clock struck the eighth chime of midnight, Columbus discovered America. During the last chime the steam engine changed the world, and in the last fraction of a second the atomic age began.

The Hemoglobin Connection

You have probably heard about blood types and other important qualities of blood. Did you ever think that your blood is like that of apemen, or *homonids,* that lived on earth 30 million years ago, or that it is like the blood of gorillas and chimpanzees?

In our blood, as in other animals, there is a substance called *hemoglobin,* the red coloring matter and oxygen carrier. Scientists who have studied this substance have learned that animals that have similar hemoglobins resemble each other. For example, members of all human races — and chimpanzees! — have identical hemoglobins.

Essential Air

Of all the vital things a body needs, air is obviously one of the most important. In the short term, it is the most important of all. A person can live two weeks without food, two days without water, but only several minutes without any air.

Workaholic

If a seventy-year-old had spent the time between age twenty and age thirty-one working continuously, that is, day and night, that person would have done as much work as most people do in their entire lives. After blowing out thirty-one candles, he or she could take a thirty-nine-year vacation.

Our Hard-working Hearts

For most of us, our days follow a cycle of eight hours at work, eight for meals and recreation, and eight for sleep. Thus, one-third of our time is spent in "rest."

The working cycle of the heart is 0.3 seconds during the contraction and 0.6 seconds of relaxation. For two-thirds of the time the heart is in a rest condition. You may think, then, that the heart is lazy, but this is not so. It has no weekends or holidays when it can "sleep late." It carries on, day and night, for seventy years or more.

Your heart does all this:

In one day it beats 100,000 times.

0.3 SECOND CONTRACTION

0.6 SECOND RELAXATION

In one year it beats 36 million times.
If you live to be eighty years old, your heart will beat 3,000 million times.

1 DAY	1 YEAR	80 YEARS
100,000 TIMES	36,000,000 TIMES	3,000 MILLION TIMES

The Blood Network

The total length of blood vessels in an adult human body is almost 1,560 miles. But the width of the greater part of this network, that of the *capillary* blood vessels — the tiniest blood vessels — is only .009 millimeter, or 1/10 the thickness of human hair. If all the blood vessels in a human body could be separated, opened, and flattened, the total area covered would be 96 square yards. 96 square yards of material would be enough to clothe 45 people.

A TV commercial for shampoo may boast that a wonderful product will make your hair strong and healthy. Usually you think of your body being strong, not your hair. But did you know that each hair can support a weight of a little more than three ounces? Three ounces may not seem like very much, but multiply it by the 100,000 hairs on most people's heads, and you will find that your hair is quite strong indeed. In fact, your hair is strong enough to support the weight of 100 of your friends if this impossible experiment were ever tried!

How Heavy Can Heavy Be?

The average weight for an adult man is 155 pounds. The heaviest man known, R.E. Hughes, tipped the scales at 1,069 pounds. He was almost seven times heavier than most men.

Get Your Hair Cut

Suppose that while you were trying hard not to gain weight, you did not cut your hair. After a year, you have successfully maintained your weight. Or so you think. But, half a pound has sneaked in. Believe it or not, this comes from your hair. Having grown about 8 inches, your hair has also put on seven ounces.

Imagine now that you're getting a haircut from a very unusual barber. He cuts only one hair at a time. How long will you be in the barber's chair? At the rate of one hair per second, the barber would take a whole day and night to cut 90,000 hairs! Since most people have more hairs, he would probably be working extra hours.

The Quick Birth of Cells

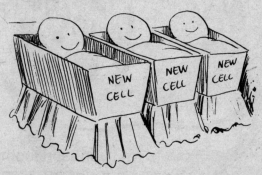

Our bodies are made of millions of cells. New cells are continuously being formed while old ones die off. The average lifespan of a human cell is about 100 days. The turnover of red blood cells is even more rapid: half of them are replaced every seven days.

The Old Cavity Story

The medical name for the enamel on teeth is *substantia adamantina* which means imperishable substance. However, as you and your friends may have learned from the dentist, enamel is hardly indestructible. It is easily broken down by sugars and acids in your mouth and this results in cavities.

You probably know that fluoride in toothpaste helps prevent cavities. For this reason, tiny amounts of fluoride are added to drinking water. It is not really dangerous as some people believe. If you drank water with fluoride for all your life, and lived seventy years, you would have consumed enough of this substance to equal just 1½ aspirin tablets a year.

Left-handed?

Whether you're a "righty" or a "lefty," have you ever wondered why most people are right-handed?

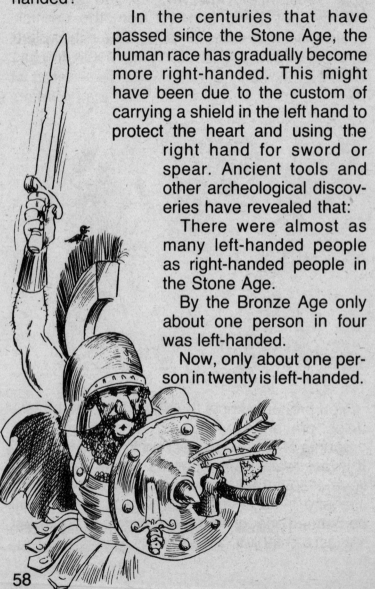

In the centuries that have passed since the Stone Age, the human race has gradually become more right-handed. This might have been due to the custom of carrying a shield in the left hand to protect the heart and using the right hand for sword or spear. Ancient tools and other archeological discoveries have revealed that:

There were almost as many left-handed people as right-handed people in the Stone Age.

By the Bronze Age only about one person in four was left-handed.

Now, only about one person in twenty is left-handed.

Chapter Six

WORDS AND BRAINY MATTERS

Growing Word Counts

Have you ever thought about how many words of the English language you know and/or use? Shakespeare's vocabulary was estimated at 24,000 words. Ancient Greek and Roman writers

had a vocabulary of only 3,000 to 9,000 words at their disposal. Language grows with time. Nowadays it expands by one word a week.

Assuming that you're an average citizen with an estimated word count of 3,000 words, you use words and terms which Shakespeare probably never imagined: television and radio, super-market and department store, car and bicycle. Perhaps you can try to list some "modern" words, especially in science. You will find that some words were unknown to your parents or grandparents when they were your age.

How's That Again?

Most people speak at a rate of 120 words per minute. However, tobacco auctioneers are known to speak at a record of 400 words per minute.

Miles of Books

In 1750 when George Washington was just beginning his military career, the National Library of Paris already contained 100,000 books. Lined up, these books would form a row three miles long. Now there are eight million books in this library. In one long row they would stretch a distance of 280 miles.

The Library of Yale University, which doubles every sixteen years, will possess in the year 2000 an estimated 200 million books. This fantastic collection would span the distance from the North Pole to the Equator.

15 — 30 — 40

Did you ever wonder how tennis got its unusual scoring system?

A first win scores 15 points.

Two wins score 30 points.

But a third win brings the score to 40 points.

Story has it that the scoring comes from the cannons on English ships that fought in the

Battle of Harfleur in 1415. The English victory was due to the help of the different cannonballs — the 15 pounders, the 30 pounders, and the 40 pounders. The evening after the battle, the victors celebrated their success with a kind of tennis game. (Tennis had its beginnings in those days.) In the game, the players used 15-30-40 scoring in honor of their cannonballs.

The Alphabet in Space

The number of ways that the twenty-six letters of our alphabet can be arranged is enormous.

If all these arrangements were written on one long piece of paper, the roll would stretch out to a length that is truly out of this world — 2,000 times the diameter of our Milky Way Galaxy!

If you used ordinary typing paper to record these arrangements, you could cover the whole earth with a layer of paper 60 miles high!

What's more, *if* these pages of paper were bound into books, and *if* you could manage to "read" them, it would take you *forever*. With an eye movement speed of 150 yards per hour, the average reader finishes a 200-page book in about six hours. The overall length of print in such a book is only a little more than half a mile. This hardly compares with even *one* diameter of the Milky Way Galaxy!